Trumpet Genius
by Leslie Gourse

A Book Report Biography
FRANKLIN WATTS
A Division of Grolier Publishing
New York / London / Hong Kong / Sydney
Danbury, Connecticut

frontispiece: Wynton Marsalis with his band
during a rehearsal in Vienna, 1996.

Cover illustration by Joan McEvoy, interpreted from a
photograph by © AP/Wide World Photos.

Photographs ©: AP/Wide World Photos. 102 (Charles Abel), 74 (Bebeto
Matthews); Archive Photos: 30 (Freddie Patterson); Corbis-Bettmann: 53
(Frank Driggs), 26, 89 (Philip Gould), 19 (Gail Mooney), 24 (Reuters),
10, 56 (UPI); Folio, Inc.: 93 (David R. Frazier); Gamma-Liaison, Inc.: 69
(Evan Agostini); Globe Photos: 94 (John Abbott); Photofest: 84 (Stephanie
Berger), 32, 52, 79; Retna Ltd./Camera Press Ltd.: 51, 65, 83 (Enid
Farber), 43 (Gary Gershoff), 22 (Eugene Gologursky), 38 (David
Redfern/Leon Morris), 2 (David Redfern), 47 (Colin Thomas), 37; Seth
Poppel Yearbook Archives: 13; Stephanie Berger: 92; Time Inc.: 71 (1990);
Time Magazine: 28 (Ted Thai).

Visit Franklin Watts on the Internet at:
http://publishing.grolier.com

Library of Congress Cataloging-in-Publication Data

Gourse, Leslie
        Wynton Marsalis : Trumpet Genius / by Leslie Gourse
        p.   cm—(A book report biography)
        Includes bibliographical references (p.) and index
        Summary: Discusses the life and musical career of the African-
American trumpet player known for his performances of popular jazz and
classical music.
        ISBN 0-531-11673-5(lib.bdg.)   ISBN 0-531-16407-1(pbk.)
        1. Marsalis, Wynton, 1961– Juvenile literature. 2. Trumpet play-
ers—United States—Biography—Juvenile literature. [1. Marsalis, Wynton. 1961– . 2. Trumpet players. 3. Afro-Americans—Biography.] I. Title. II.
Series.
        ML3930.M327G68 1999
        788.9'2'092-dc21
        [B]   99-10605
                                                                                    CIP

CONTENTS

This is the story of trumpeter Wynton Learson Marsalis, who rose to become one of the most famous and influential jazz and classical musicians in the modern world. When he was only 22 years old, he became the first jazz musician to win Grammy awards in both jazz and classical music. Grammys are the highest awards in the recording industry. Before he was 30, Wynton became artistic director of Jazz at Lincoln Center, the most prestigious arts center in the world. At age 36, he won the Pulitzer Prize, the highest award given to artists in America—and it was the first time a Pulitzer went to a jazz musician. Supposedly it was for his jazz oratorio, *Blood on the Fields*, a work combining words and music and inspired by the history of slavery. But actually the Pulitzer recognized all the good work Wynton had done during his career.

In 1984, Wynton won a Grammy for "Best Jazz Instrumental Performance, Soloist."

These accomplishments may seem to indicate that Wynton has lived a charmed life, but he has worked hard to win his honors. He has endured much more than his fair share of criticism. Some of it came from people who did not share his traditional taste in music. Other critics simply had less vision than Wynton. And some people envied him because no one else in jazz history has ever been so rich, famous, and praised so early in life.

Wynton has handled all his challenges by concentrating on his work. He has the strength of character to work harder and longer hours than nearly anyone else and to inspire others to follow his example. His father, Ellis Marsalis, Jr., a well-known jazz pianist and teacher in New Orleans—Wynton's hometown—has been a wonderful role model and advisor for Wynton and his brothers. Learning from his father, Wynton developed the desire to spread the word about the greatness and grandeur of jazz. And above all else in life, he has always loved to play music. As he once told a journalist, "When I play the trumpet, all my troubles disappear." These passions are the secret of his success.

"When I play the trumpet, all my troubles disappear."

CHAPTER ONE

WYNTON SETS OUT ON HIS OWN

In 1978, when Wynton Marsalis graduated from high school in New Orleans, Louisiana, he looked like an ordinary, slender, 17-year-old adolescent. He usually wore blue jeans, heavy-rimmed glasses, and a big Afro that bounced when he walked. But he had already won a number of awards for his trumpet playing. He was the first African-American to win first prize in an important competition. It opened doors for him to play in several classical music orchestras in New Orleans. And he had decided to go North to study trumpet. His elder brother, Branford, a saxophonist, had already left home to study in Boston.

"I just loved to play the trumpet."

When Wynton was 12 years old, he started practicing the trumpet—morning, noon, and night.

Wynton impressed his teachers ever since he was in junior high school.

The exercises were difficult and boring, but they improved his playing. Wynton's technique became astounding. "I just loved to play the trumpet," he said. He and Branford had led a funk group for dances and parties throughout their teen years.

Branford was talented, but he didn't like to practice as much as Wynton did. Branford called Wynton "the best trumpet player in the South."

Coming from a family rich in musical talent but short of money, Wynton didn't even own a suitcase. His mother wanted him to go to college in Louisiana. But Wynton, who had won scholarships to many Ivy League schools, had a different dream. He packed a box with a few pairs of pants, shirts, tapes of music, and a stereo recorder, and headed for New York City. He wanted to audition for the Juilliard School, a world-famous music conservatory.

Wynton arrived for his audition at the school's campus at the Lincoln Center arts complex. Its magnificent concert and opera halls and theater were built around an elegant fountain. On Juilliard's bulletin board, Wynton saw an announcement for scholarship auditions for the Tanglewood Music Festival at Lenox, Massachusetts. He decided to try for that, too. It would give him a chance to spend the summer listening, playing, and studying with great musicians.

The Tanglewood auditions took place in a hotel near Lincoln Center. Gunther Schuller, a renowned authority on jazz and classical music, and president of the famed New England Conservatory in Boston, was one of the judges. They asked Wynton to play a variety of pieces. "The most spectacular thing he played were excerpts from the *Brandenburg Concerto Number Two*, a famous trumpet piece, which no one in my 22 years at Tanglewood ever dared to play at an audition, because it's death," recalled Schuller. Among its other demands, the piece has very high notes. "Nobody makes it. And he did. He played it flawlessly."

Wynton would later explain his fearless attitude about that challenge. "It's a distinct possibility to fail to play it, and be one of many who failed." Though he hadn't failed, "You never know when you're going to fail. That's just a part

> **"You never know when you're going to fail. That's just a part of succeeding—failing."**

of succeeding—failing. And it's not that big a deal. It's something to laugh about. You can pick yourself up and go on tomorrow," he explained. "That's the beauty of it. That's how you succeed."

But Tanglewood required that scholarship students be at least 18 years old. Wynton was only 17, but Schuller didn't care. "If he was three and a half, I would take him," he told the other judges. "My God, a beautiful, young, fresh talent." Schuller found out that Wynton also played jazz and was "spectacular" at that too, Schuller said. Then Wynton won a four-year scholarship to Juilliard to begin in the fall.

"My God, a beautiful, young, fresh talent."

With other summer scholarship students at Tanglewood, Wynton lived in a prep-school dorm set in an area of fresh air, rolling hills, and huge trees. Wynton played his horn constantly and always asked questions about music and life. "His eyes observed everybody. People at Tanglewood have that attitude, a good attitude, discipline, and great pride to be part of the festival," recalled Eiji Oue, a conducting student from Japan. He would always have a vivid memory of Wynton "blowing, blowing, oh my God, he made me upset, mad sometimes." Wynton woke Oue up at night. "He played the same thing over and over. One night I was dreaming and screaming in my dream, 'Wrong note!' I believe it was a Stravinsky piece called *Petroushka*. He had to practice the solos, and sometimes they were difficult. He practiced at 5 and 6 A.M." At Tanglewood, Wynton became best friends with trumpeter Justin Cohen, of Buffalo, New York. Justin, too, noticed how much Wynton practiced. "Like most great musicians, he practiced until he got it perfect," Justin said, "and then he played it over and over the right way to reinforce it. Anytime you hear someone play the trumpet very well, you know he has worked hard," said Justin.

Wynton would later explain that he was trying to master technique. Then he could express himself and his individual personality through music.

Wynton and Justin played in an orchestra and gave weekly pops and jazz concerts. They also studied with the Boston Symphony musicians, who played a separate program on weekends. And in their free time, Wynton and Justin discussed the racial situation in America. Justin had never met anyone before who talked a great deal about race. "What the hell did I know, growing up in the suburbs of Buffalo, about being African-American in this country?" Justin said. "He shared with me . . . He made me aware of it . . . and it wasn't the legal segregation. It was the way people look at you when you're in a store." In a store one day, Wynton called Justin's attention to a clerk's reaction just because of Wynton's race. "It was great to have my eyes opened [to] the prejudice that is inherent in America," Justin said.

At Tanglewood, Wynton met drummer Akira Tana, a New England Conservatory graduate, who played both jazz and classical music. He and Wynton worked a few nights in clubs with an experienced jazz bass player who spent summers in the area. Wynton already knew a great deal about jazz, because his father, Ellis Marsalis, was a highly respected jazz pianist and teacher at the New Orleans Center for the Creative Arts—NOCCA. Talented kids studied there in the afternoons. Ellis gave all his students, including his sons, invaluable lessons in music and about life, too.

At home, Ellis played his jazz records for his sons all the time. At first, they preferred pop music. And Wynton loved classical music most of all. Slowly Wynton began falling in love with jazz, mostly because he admired his father so much. Ellis always encouraged his sons and all his students to practice. And if they wanted to play music as their life's work, he told them to commit themselves wholeheartedly to it. He didn't want them to study a subject just to have something to fall back on.

At Tanglewood, Jim Tinsley, an African-American trumpeter who sometimes played with the Boston Symphony, heard Wynton play. Tinsley was very impressed. Wynton won a citation at the festival. So Tinsley telephoned his friend, Wilmer Wise, an African-American classical trumpeter in New York, and told him, "There's a kid coming to New York. I'm floored by his abilities. If there's anything you can do to help him, please do."

In the fall, Wynton and Akira Tana shared an apartment on the Upper West Side of New York

City. Wynton went to Wilmer Wise's apartment to play for the older trumpeter. "He was absolutely incredible," Wise recalled. "I hadn't heard many players of any age who played as well." Wise helped Wynton find jobs in Broadway show orchestras, classical music groups, and even with a band that toured Mexico.

Though Wynton liked studying classical music at Juilliard, he was becoming more convinced that he wanted to be a jazz musician. He had very definite ideas about jazz. He didn't want

The Juilliard School in New York City

to play fusion—jazz with electronic instruments. He kept going to clubs and sitting in with acoustic jazz groups. Older jazz musicians were so impressed that they started calling him for jobs. And Wynton spent all his time listening, practicing, and working at music.

He remained friendly with Justin Cohen, his schoolmate at Juilliard. They often went to jazz clubs and classical concerts together. Justin said, "For some people, doing what they love is like breathing." That was Wynton, he said.

"For some people, doing what they love is like breathing."

CHAPTER TWO

WYNTON SPREADS HIS WINGS

At the end of the 1970s, rock music was the most popular music in the United States. Rock-jazz fusion, with electronic instruments, had many fans. Trumpeter Miles Davis had popularized the blending, or fusion, of acoustic and electronic instruments in 1969 with his album, *Bitches Brew*. (The musicians in the group called each other "bitches" when they contributed something especially good to the album.) By the time Wynton arrived in New York, acoustic jazz hadn't been popular for about 20 years. And Wynton wanted to play only acoustic music, as his father had done as a struggling pianist in New Orleans.

Akira Tana told Wynton he should try to work for the Jazz Messengers, a brilliant acoustic group led by the old bebop drummer Art Blakey. He was a disciple of Dizzy Gillespie—a founder of the sophisticated, complex style of modern music

Ellis Marsalis at the piano

known as bebop. Akira told Wynton, "Art Blakey's is the only band out here that you can play with. It's your last chance, your last hope to learn how to play." Akira took Wynton to meet Blakey when the Jazz Messengers worked at a Manhattan club. Wynton sat in with the group. He was wearing a cotton windbreaker jacket on that cold winter night, one of Blakey's musicians noticed. Even though Wynton didn't know how to play Blakey's repertoire well, the group's pianist, James Williams, was impressed by Wynton's command of the trumpet. "I heard something special," Williams recalled. Blakey invited Wynton to sit in again.

The next day, Williams visited Wynton to practice Blakey's repertoire. Wynton took a bus to Boston to sit in with Blakey's group the next weekend. Wynton's brother Branford, who was at the Berklee College of Music in Boston, gave Wynton a place to stay.

It was clear, from his eerie tone and phrasing, that Wynton had been greatly influenced by Miles Davis's recordings. They were made in the 1960s, when Miles had been leading great acoustic groups. Wynton had a lot to learn about other historic jazz trumpeters. He kept studying. And it seemed likely that Wynton would soon join Blakey.

Wynton called his father in New Orleans and said he was thinking about quitting Juilliard and going on the road with Blakey. "I knew myself I wanted to play," Wynton would recall. "But I always talked to my daddy to see what he was thinking. I knew before I asked him that he was going to say 'go and play.' My daddy believes in playing . . . Some

> **"I knew myself I wanted to play, but I always talked to my daddy to see what he was thinking."**

Miles Davis and Wynton had their differences about jazz rock fusion, which Miles played later in his life.

people think you should take the safe road. He's not like that. His idea is—go out there and do it. If you fail it, you tried it. Don't stay at home. Don't be afraid. You don't have nothing. Don't worry. You never had nothing. So you don't have to worry about losing nothing. You can always go back to what you did."

By the summer of 1980, Wynton was playing in a hard-swinging, bebop style with Art Blakey and traveling all over the United States, Japan, and Europe. While learning from Blakey, Wynton actually taught lessons about self-confidence and discipline to his fellow band members. For example, if you want to learn something, it can take a year or a minute. It depends on the limits you put on yourself. "He showed me the power of the mind," said Bobby Watson, Blakey's alto saxophonist.

Wynton always attributed his readiness to face the world as his legacy from his father. Wynton's mother, Dolores Marsalis, was a teacher who stayed home to bring up her family of six sons, run the house, and give them standards. She wouldn't tolerate them becoming troublemakers. One night, Wynton and a friend sneaked cigarettes in a frame of a house being built in the neighborhood. Accidentally, they set the frame on fire. Dolores pulled Wynton's pants down in the street and spanked him in front of the neighbors.

Wynton's mother, Dolores, was a strong influence on his character and on his music studies.

Wynton was humiliated, and he was shocked at how angry she was.

At the same time, Wynton observed his father's steadfast devotion to jazz. Ellis worked for low fees in clubs. On the side, he took teaching jobs. He had a bachelor's degree, and then he studied for a master's degree. But at one point, he had so little money that he was thinking about getting a job as a taxi driver. Dolores told him to keep playing the piano. There had been professional musicians in her family with its roots deep in New Orleans. One uncle had played bass with the great Duke Ellington band. Wynton was impressed by his mother's understanding of Ellis's love for music. That's when Wynton, at age 12, began practicing all the time.

Wynton's brother Branford was born on August 26, 1960. Then 14 months later, on October 18, 1961, Wynton was born. The family lived in Kenner, a racially mixed but segregated community just across the railroad tracks from New Orleans. Branford and Wynton went to an officially integrated, but mostly white, Catholic school. Their father was Protestant, but Dolores had been raised a Catholic.

Dolores made sure the children had music lessons and took part in community activities. Many were affiliated with the church. Wynton played in kids' groups—the Jesuit Honor Band, for one, when he was 10, and the Fairview Baptist Church Band under the leadership of Danny Barker, an eminent New Orleans guitarist and banjoist. Without realizing it at the time, Wynton learned important lessons about New Orleans's jazz legacy. He also learned about stagecraft and poise in front of audiences.

Other Marsalis children were born—first Ellis III in 1964, then Delfeayo, who was named for Dolores's brother, in 1965. In 1970, another brother, Mboya, was born. But Mboya didn't talk; he walked on tiptoes, and he kept hitting his head, and he threw his food on the floor. "There's something wrong with that boy," Wynton said, though he didn't really know. When Mboya was

The Marsalis family at home. From the left are Dolores, Mboya, Ellis, Delfeayo, and Jason.

two years old, he was diagnosed with autism. Dolores kept him home to take care of him.

In 1974, the family had a change of fortune. Ellis was hired to teach music to high school students in a new school called the New Orleans Center for the Creative Arts, which was nicknamed NOCCA. Many talented kids studied sight-singing and ear training and played in a jazz ensemble with Ellis. Ellis discovered he had a special gift as an educator. An unusual proportion of Ellis's students became serious about playing music for their careers. And all of them praised Ellis for his guidance about music and life.

In those days, Wynton and Branford were very close. "We did a lot of stuff together," Wynton recalled. "We rode our bikes together all over the city. We lived in the same room. We both played music."

Branford started The Creators, a funk music group, and wanted Wynton to play in it. Wynton refused, because he thought pop music was too loud and simple. So Branford asked his father to force Wynton to join The Creators. Wynton obeyed and loved playing with Branford. They had a special communion. "We worked on playing together all the time," Wynton recalled. "Branford has quick reflexes and can hear real good, and we knew each other's playing. He was always in tune. He would learn music real fast."

Brothers Branford (left) and Wynton played together for years, but Branford decided to set out on his own.

Despite the fun they had playing for dances and meeting girls, Wynton preferred European classical music. He fell in love with a classical recording by a great French trumpeter, Maurice Andre. Wynton knew he wanted to play like Andre. Wynton slowly grew to appreciate jazz—the complex, swinging music that his father loved. Wynton had been named after Wynton Kelly, a wonderful jazz pianist who had played in

Miles Davis's bebop-rooted group. Ellis played bebop and other modern jazz recordings for his sons all the time. The exposure finally had an impact on Wynton.

Then a jazz song, probably the lyrical "Cousin Mary," played by the innovative jazz saxophonist John Coltrane on his album, *Giant Steps*, caught Wynton's attention. Wynton played that record over and over again. He chose it from his father's collection because of its serious-looking cover with a bit of red and white decoration. Ellis's other albums had photographs of women and people in costumes.

In this case, the album cover said something about the music. Coltrane's music communicated a strong spirituality—a yearning—an upward, high-minded striving. Wynton became enamored of Coltrane's power and learned many of his songs by ear from recordings.

Neither Ellis nor Dolores Marsalis tried to push the children to play music professionally or to aim for greatness. Dolores hadn't even pushed Wynton to become an altar boy in the Catholic Church. Branford had agreed to become one. Wynton was fascinated with the story of Jesus's life, and he believed in Jesus. But he didn't like the way whites and blacks sat in separate sections in church. So when he was eight, he refused to be an

John Coltrane's distinctive saxophone style helped Wynton fall in love with jazz.

altar boy. He felt that some aspects of religion were "too much anti-people," he said. He was learning to think for himself.

His parents didn't give the children any choice about the importance of education, however. Dolores sent Branford and Wynton to New

Orleans to high school together, because she wanted them to look out for each other. Soon the whole family moved to New Orleans, taking over a house that Ellis's father put up for sale there. Wynton kept getting deeper into music. He loved basketball and would always play it well for recreation. But most of all, he adored playing the trumpet. "That was just what I wanted to do," he said. "It was just something I could relate to. It was fun."

Occasionally, Wynton ran into problems with racism in school. One teacher denied him a prize for having the highest mark in his class because she wanted a white child to have the honor. When Wynton asked her about it, she said the award wasn't based just on the mark. But Wynton knew it was supposed to be. However, there was nothing he could do about it. Most other teachers treated him with fairness. And at home Wynton was always nurtured by his parents. He looked up to both of them. "My father could play any tune in any key . . . I just wanted to be like him. I just wanted to be cool." Wynton loved the feeling of hipness in clubs. "My father was so hip . . . very laid back and cool and never

"My father could play any tune in any key . . . I just wanted to be like him. I just wanted to be cool."

excited. You didn't see him get mad. He knew about a lot of stuff, too." He knew about baseball, automobiles, and politics. "We'd go to the barber shop . . . They would be talking about politics. My dad would be breaking it down. He knew a lot about the world. And he had a lot of books."

When Ellis went to hear Wynton and Branford play their pop music gigs, Ellis encouraged them, saying, "Yeah, man, you all sound nice." Ellis never complained.

In his sophomore year, Wynton won a concerto competition. It was the first time an African-American had been a winner in that competition. It led to his performing the *Haydn Trumpet Concerto* with the New Orleans Philharmonic. Ellis found many fine teachers for Wynton. He began playing with the New Orleans Civic Orchestra and the New Orleans Philharmonic Symphony brass quintet. He was only 16 when he performed the *Brandenburg Concerto No. 2 in F Major* with the New Orleans Philharmonic.

It was hard for him to overcome his resentment of the European classical music world, where whites did not welcome African-American musicians to play. But "I had to succumb to the

"I had to succumb to the greatness of the music."

greatness of the music," Wynton would later recall. And he heeded the advice of older people who told him he needed to get an education, be a part of the world, and appreciate its cultural riches.

His father always insisted the children acquire information to back up their opinions. The right to free speech didn't mean that the children had a right to say whatever they felt like saying. They had the right only to an informed opinion. He insisted that they know what they were doing when they played music, too. They couldn't play anything that just happened to come into their heads. That wasn't freedom.

When he was 15 and 16, Wynton auditioned and won scholarships to the Eastern Music Festival, a classical festival in North Carolina. "We didn't have a lot of money. So I got scholarships to everything," Wynton recalled. "I was basically good in everything in school . . . My main strength was integrating the material, seeing how things related to everything else. I always liked the way math, language, and science related to each other."

At the Eastern Music Festival, Wynton learned a great deal from other students and older professional musicians. He won other music scholarships in New Orleans. And at NOCCA, Wynton took charge of a brass quartet. His father thought Wynton bossed the other kids around too much, but another teacher didn't think so. Wynton was just trying to make the music as good as it could possibly be.

From that time on, some people would call Wynton "bossy," while others would think he was simply self-confident. Wynton's mother noticed that Wynton always wanted things to go the way he said they should. But everyone admired Wynton's capacity for long hours of hard work.

He kept preparing himself for a life in music. When Wynton complained once to Ellis that a gig they had played together wasn't much fun, and the audience had been small, Ellis told him, "That's how it always is. If you want to play, that's how you have to want to play. This gig here, this is every gig . . . It can be a gig where the people are cheering and screaming, or it can be this gig right here." From Ellis, Wynton learned to celebrate every gig.

In 1976, Dolores had her sixth and last child, Jason. Branford went away to college the next year. Wynton missed Branford terribly but kept himself busy with music. He and a trumpet-playing friend, Terence Blanchard, who would also become a star one day, loved Miles Davis, Clifford Brown, Clark Terry, Woody Shaw, and Freddie Hubbard—all great jazz trumpeters.

Wynton actually earned quite a bit of money from his jobs in funk groups and classical orches-

*Wynton (left) and his friend, trumpeter
Terence Blanchard*

tras—more money than Ellis earned from his
jazz gigs. Wynton put the money right back into
music, buying a variety of trumpets. He didn't buy
clothes. Many girls found him attractive, because
he could play so well and talk so charmingly. But
one girl who liked him a lot recalled how short his
jeans were. Clothes weren't important to him then.

Although Wynton loved Ellis III and Delfeayo, his younger brothers were brought up in a
buddy system with each other as Wynton and

Branford had been. Ellis III and Delfeayo were closer to each other than they were to Wynton. Ellis III played the guitar a little, and Delfeayo chose the trombone. So all of them were musical. But Ellis III was never really serious about playing the guitar. Wynton tried to be kind to Mboya and spent time with him. But he felt closest to Branford.

Jason, who played the drums with great and obvious talent when he was a boy, was only two years old when Wynton went to college and joined Art Blakey. It would be a while before Wynton knew Jason half as well as he knew his fellow musicians in the Jazz Messengers.

Marsalis brothers Jason (left) and Delfeayo

CHAPTER THREE

WYNTON BECOMES A STAR

From his playing in the classical music world, Wynton brought a certain amount of discipline and rigidity to Blakey's band. His background enabled him to contribute good ideas to the Messengers about how to present music. He also brought along youthful exuberance and kept the other fellows on their toes because he played so well. "He had a natural gift for getting audiences involved in his solos . . . He picked up the trumpet and played the hell out of it," one musician remembered. After a while, Wynton found a job for his brother Branford in the band.

Wynton was still working out a lot of things in his music and his life, and he asked for advice from other people. From Blakey, Wynton learned such things as how to pace himself, build solos, and play ballads better—"things that old guys always know more about than young guys do," said one of the band members. "All of us owe Art." Wynton actually worried about his future, as all the other fellows in the band did. Would he be successful? Would he make any statements about himself and jazz?

To guide his musicians, Blakey told them to write music and use the royalties as a legacy for their children. Blakey wanted his musicians to grow and lead their own bands. And he preached: "Be true to yourself. Whatever you are, you be it, and be it all the way, because nothing else is going to work anyway."

> **"Be true to yourself. Whatever you are, you be it, and be it all the way, because nothing else is going to work anyway."**

Wynton became especially friendly with the band's bassist, Charles Fambrough. They shared hotel rooms on tours, Fambrough said, "because Wynton was very personable, energetic, and he always wanted to make the music sound as good as it could possibly sound." Fambrough got Wynton interested in buying nice clothes to wear for work. Wynton's hours of practicing and studying paid off for him. In *Down Beat* magazine's critics' poll for 1981—a traditional barometer of the popularity of musicians—Wynton was chosen the Talent Deserving Wider Recognition. Donald Brown, a pianist who joined the band when James Williams left, liked to write music. He and Wynton sometimes discussed composing. Each time Wynton wrote a tune, Donald heard improvement.

Fambrough observed that Wynton was constantly developing ideas by listening to a lot of other musicians. He also noticed that Branford and Wynton were close, except that Wynton often tried to tell Branford what to do. Branford didn't like that. "Branford was very cool. He didn't need anyone telling him what to do. He did the opposite of what Wynton told him to do." Fambrough thought that was fairly normal behavior for siblings. Younger kids often like to tell the older ones what to do, and the older ones never listen.

But the Marsalis brothers stuck together. Fambrough recalled telling them that New Orleans musicians "weren't all that much." The brothers tussled with Fambrough. The fight wasn't serious, but it showed Fambrough that the brothers didn't let other people upset their bonds of family and background. Other musicians also noticed that the Marsalis brothers often stepped up to defend each other if anybody threatened one of them.

Around this time, Columbia Records was reissuing old jazz recordings, trying to fill the void in the music world left by rock concerts. Rock concerts had become dangerous. Fights often broke out and parents didn't want their children getting hurt. The old jazz records by musicians such as Miles Davis began selling again. Record company executives wanted to find a way to make jazz even more popular.

Bruce Lundvall, president of Columbia Records, heard Wynton play when he sat in with trumpeter Woody Shaw's group at Fat Tuesday, a New York jazz club. Lundvall, who had signed Shaw to Columbia, now became very enthusiastic about Wynton. After the set, Lundvall told Wynton, "I'd like to sign you to Columbia Records." The next day, Lundvall and a lawyer from the company met with Wynton and a lawyer. "And we signed him," Lundvall recalled. He told George Butler, in charge of jazz at Columbia, that the company had signed Wynton. Butler took charge of Wynton's recording schedule.

Suddenly Wynton had the chance, at age 20, to lead his own group and record for a major record label. Some people objected to Columbia signing him, because they thought other, older jazz musicians deserved a chance. But Columbia wanted Wynton for his youth, talent, and attractive looks. Soon Columbia found out he also played classical music, and the company signed him to record that, too. Blakey had always told his musicians to stay in a place until they had learned all the lessons they possibly could. Wynton may have been able to learn more from

Blakey, but he couldn't travel all over the world with Blakey and with his own group, too. So he had to quit Blakey's group.

Branford left Blakey to help Wynton organize a quintet. Wynton asked Branford to switch from

Jeff Watts and Wynton take a rehearsal break

alto to tenor saxophone, and Branford did that for the new group. A very talented young pianist named Kenny Kirkland, born in 1935, had a mid-Manhattan loft where young players gathered at night to talk and jam—play informally. Branford, who had heard him play, asked Kenny, a Manhattan School of Music student, to join Wynton's group. Kenny was clearly under the influence of star pianist Herbie Hancock's style. Hancock had played in a famous Miles Davis group in the 1960s. Branford also asked drummer Jeff Watts, born in 1960, to come along. And two bassists were hired. One was Clarence Seay, and the other was Wynton's friend Charles Fambrough. Seay played on the group's first recording, "We Three Kings of Orient Are," for a record called *God Rest Ye, Merry Jazzmen,* in June 1981 in New York City. Both bassists played for Wynton's first jazz album in 1982, *Wynton Marsalis.*

Wynton played with his group in New York and on the road. He began to meet many people everywhere, fans and budding musicians among them. Sometimes he gave lessons to young musicians who showed up backstage. He spent hours with them, gave them his phone number in New York, and often kept in touch with them to find out about their progress. Eventually, he hired some of them or found jobs for them.

"People really accepted it," Kenny Kirkland

remembered about the quintet years later. "The work was strong." He realized it helped promote a resurgence of interest in jazz. Wynton was playing bebop and looking for logical ways to develop the classic jazz style. He was making inroads against the dominance of rock and fusion.

The quintet's first record was nominated for a Grammy. Though the record didn't win, it made Wynton aware of what a Grammy was. The critics praised him, particularly for his tone. Some people said he had a cold sound from his classical background, and others thought he was too young and inexperienced for all the acclaim. Still others were jealous of him. But the majority of the reviews from important critics boosted him. New Orleans Mayor Ernest Morial proclaimed a Wynton Marsalis Day in February 1982.

A notable critic, Chris Albertson, wrote about Wynton's first album: "There's not a blemish on it."[1] Other reviews in important publications, ranging from the *Village Voice* to *The New York Times*, had fine things to say about Wynton and his group. One critic in a New York paper, the *Post*, said, "Wynton is classically trained, disciplined, with a large, warm tone and a sense of phrase shape and placement rare these days in one his age. . . . Wynton and Branford . . . seem to be at the center of a circle of young, highly skilled players determined to find their inspiration across the entire history of their music . . . the music is delicious."[2]

In 1982, Wynton won both the Musician of the Year award and the Best Trumpeter award in *Down Beat* magazine polls. He beat both Miles Davis and Dizzy Gillespie, the leading older jazz trumpeters.

Soon there would be trouble between Wynton and Miles. Who threw the first stone? Probably it was Wynton. He criticized electronic music, which Miles was playing exclusively by then. Wynton was very outspoken, criticizing many older, famous musicians. He thought New Orleans music was "a museum piece," he told one critic. Young musicians shouldn't be playing it. He wasn't fond of the blues, or Dizzy Gillespie, or even Louis Armstrong, whom Wynton called an "Uncle Tom," because he emphasized smiling and entertaining. Even so, Wynton's career kept making strides. His fame overrode the harsh things he was saying.

He and Branford made a critically praised record, *Fathers and Sons*, with their father Ellis. And, on the road, Wynton worked hard to make life go smoothly for his group. He fought for good conditions in hotels and clubs. "For a jazz gig, it was a blessing," Kenny Kirkland said.

Columbia's publicity department tried hard to launch Wynton. Marilyn Laverty, the publicist assigned to him, set up interviews with the press, and Wynton kept all the dates. He was so cooperative and friendly that she thought he was a dream artist. And tickets for his quintet's concerts

At 21, Wynton was already considered the "Prince of Jazz."

sold well. Young women stood in front of posters advertising him and said, "Isn't he cute?" He had a neat, short hairstyle. He sported round, preppy-looking glasses. And he wore well-tailored suits. There was a clean-cut, all-American look to the young prodigy.

He would eventually tell Ed Bradley, an interviewer for the CBS show "60 Minutes" on November 26, 1995, that he wanted to be well dressed for his audiences. And if it turned out that he wasn't playing well enough, they could say, "Well, at least he was clean." Audiences loved his sense of humor.

His long-playing records sold so well that other jazz labels went scurrying in search of more, talented, little Wyntons. He had given jazz the final shot in the arm that it needed for commercial attention. He became so successful so quickly that other young players set their sights on careers in acoustic jazz. Even so, Wynton told a journalist that his life was no bed of roses. "You have to think of something to play all the time. That's pressure. You get assigned a personality by the media that's not yours. There's the business aspect. Everyone's trying to make as much money off you as possible. And you have to try to play jazz and go on the road with a group, with all the responsibility. That's hard."[3]

Wynton and Branford were interviewed for a cover story of *Down Beat* magazine in December 1982. They talked about the creativity of the quintet's members. Branford told the interviewer for the article that he was learning by watching Wynton do all the work of handling the business people. That story was supposedly about the two brothers. But it really featured Wynton, 21, more than Branford, 22. And the seeds of a rift between the brothers were being sown.

Branford had his own contract with Columbia by then. He wasn't going to hire Wynton for the group, because Branford didn't want to be overshadowed by his more famous brother. The brothers sometimes argued and contradicted each other. Branford liked to play pop music, and Wynton didn't even particularly like to listen to it. But in some ways they were two peas in a pod. Both revered jazz traditions. But Branford didn't criticize other musicians as much as Wynton did. Branford didn't step on toes. And he didn't like pressure or hard work as much as Wynton did. Branford described himself as "lazy."

But both of them seemed to echo their father's standards in many ways. Wynton said, "Music goes forward. Music doesn't go backwards. Whatever the cats couldn't play before you, you're supposed to play." And Branford added, "There's a huge movement for the perpetuation of ignorance in jazz. Play. That's all."

And so they progressed beyond their quibbling and teasing and wound up nearly finishing each other's sentences.

_____

"There's a huge movement for the perpetuation of ignorance in jazz. Play. That's all."

_____

Both had their own ways of concentrating on their careers. Years later, Branford would reflect upon that interview and say they had followed the individual paths they talked about at that time.

Wynton hadn't liked it when Branford contradicted him. They argued later about having argued during that interview. Wynton would reflect that he had always been aware of some sibling rivalry with Branford. They had a very complex relationship. It was fraught with competition, but there was also a profound and enduring love and loyalty on both sides. Never would they be free of their bond, nor would they ever want to be free. The bond would override many storms—quarrels between themselves, and sometimes quarrels between one of them and the rest of the world. In a true crisis, Branford usually stood steadfast on the side of his brother, and Wynton did the same.

Wynton began to forge new, close relation-

Early in their careers, Branford (right) and Wynton
often shared the stage.

ships as his career blossomed. A critic for the *Village Voice* newspaper, Stanley Crouch, who particularly liked Wynton's playing, befriended the young man and told him about the beauties of Louis Armstrong's music and Duke Ellington's, too. Wynton had never thought much about the early jazz masters and didn't realize how complex their music was. Stanley gave him records and introduced him to Albert Murray, an even older

Louis Armstrong

man and a staunch lover of the old masters. Murray, a writer, had known the masters personally. Duke and Count Basie had been his friends. Murray, too, gave Wynton advice about what to read and listen to. Gradually Wynton got a well-rounded education in world culture.

Crouch even cooked meals for Wynton. A great lover of food, Crouch made much better meals than Wynton could cook for himself. And Crouch, a complicated, virtually self-educated man who had grown up in Watts, an African-American community in Los Angeles, was very understanding. Wynton could confide in him.

Duke Ellington

They discussed music endlessly and talked about what annoyed them on the scene so filled with pop and electronic music, and with sometimes chaotic, experimental, avant-garde music too. Wynton began to develop the highest regard for Armstrong and Ellington. "Because more than any other musician's, [Armstrong's] sound carries the feeling and meaning of jazz. Anything you want, he has it—warmth and intelligence, worldly and provincial, spiritual and tawdry, down-home but sophisticated. The most complex player there's ever been, yet he can still sound like a country boy," Wynton said. His mistaken ideas were fast disappearing.

And Wynton found a girlfriend. Having dinner one night with a doctor friend in a Brooklyn restaurant, Wynton noticed a very attractive girl come in with her father. Wynton's friend knew the girl. He and Wynton sat down with Candace Stanley and her father, an architect. Soon, she and Wynton began dating. Their friends realized the two were in love. She liked music, though she was not a musician; she worked with computers. But Wynton admired the tall, slender girl with quiet style. She was a great dancer, too, Wynton found out.

Throughout the 1980s, he and Candace carried on a complicated love affair. She wanted a stable, committed relationship, their friends said. Wynton was a free spirit. Many girls chased after him in New York and on the road. But music came first in his life. Nobody and nothing could matter more. "He was completely focused on music," said one woman, who became his close friend.

Wynton's career kept becoming brighter. He played in concerts with such stars as tenor saxophonist Sonny Rollins. Wynton also made highly praised recordings of classical music, and he was declared one of the greatest classical trumpeters who had ever lived. His dream of playing like the French trumpet master Maurice Andre had become a reality. *The New York Times* critics praised virtually every performance and recording that Wynton did—classical and jazz—and that paper was the most influential in the world.

With his quintet, Wynton won his first two Grammys. One was for *Think of One,* his second jazz album, on which the brilliance of his playing was reconfirmed. It contained such tunes as "Knozz Moe King" (No Smoking). The second Grammy was for the classical *Concert for Trumpet and Orchestra in E Flat Major* by L. Mozart. Both albums were recorded in 1983. In his acceptance speech for his jazz Grammy, Wynton spoke out against electronic music. So everyone became aware of the blazing intensity of his opinions and his criticisms of Miles Davis. Wynton began to make enemies among musicians who didn't like to hear Wynton criticize Miles. For his accomplishments, Miles was regarded as a god by many jazz musicians and fans. Some musicians even stopped talking to Wynton. Miles began criticizing Wynton to the press too.

In 1984, Wynton recorded his third jazz quintet album, *Hot House Flowers,* and for that he won his second jazz Grammy. He was getting far more attention than Branford in the media. Wynton was constantly working harder and longer than anyone else. "He would just lead by example and would be tough on himself. That would give you a

Wynton accepts his 1984 Grammy award

certain amount of inspiration," said Jeff Watts, the quintet's drummer.

In July 1984, Wynton was on the cover of *Down Beat* magazine alone. In many ways, he was humble in his statements about himself. He never bragged. He still criticized pop music and the avant-garde. And he wanted to encourage young musicians to play acoustic traditional jazz, because he just adored jazz.

He said the most important thing in jazz is "swing. Rhythm. If it don't swing, I don't want to hear it; it's not important to hear whatever it is if it's not swinging, if it's jazz. There are different feelings of swing, but if it's swinging, you know it . . . ." His pronouncements were reminiscent of Duke Ellington's famous adage: "It don't mean a thing if it ain't got that swing." Wynton called his band members "the greatest young musicians on the scene." And he said he stayed up all night playing music because he loved it. "Now you can say what you want to say. I've got such strong opinions because I love the music."

"I've got such strong opinions because I love the music."

Gary Giddins, a prize-winning critic for the *Village Voice*, tried to stress Wynton's importance: "His contribution is of another kind—consolidation, interpretation, popularization. . . . Don't be so hard on the guy just because he's getting the attention lots of jazz musicians should get." In other words, Wynton was calling attention to the well-established mainstream style of classic jazz created by the masters from the start of the 1900s up through the mid-1960s.

In January 1985, Wynton led his group in an album, *Black Codes from the Underground*. It wasn't the kind of spontaneous improvisation that the avant-garde played. But this intense album, from the first cut, which was the title tune, showed the influence of Wynton's study of modernists and experimentalists. He presented an open style of music. A listener could sing a note and blend in with any of the songs; they had the feeling of modal music. And on his solos, Wynton had spectacular power. The fiery album became the favorite of Wynton's projects among some experimentalists and modernists. They were delighted when it won a Grammy.

Wynton's next album, too, *J Mood*, also a Grammy winner, reflected his modernist bent. He included the song "Insane Asylum" by his old friend Donald Brown. Like *Black Codes from the Underground*, the music showcased Wynton as a brilliant trumpeter and exploratory mainstream player. But *J Mood*, recorded in December 1985, constituted a major departure from Wynton's earlier albums. It was more mellow than *Black Codes*. And Branford didn't play on *J Mood*. Neither did Kenny Kirkland.

The two had quit Wynton's band because they wanted to play with Sting, a British pop singer and bassist. They were willing to keep playing with Wynton, but they didn't agree to fit Wynton's busy schedule into Sting's busy schedule. However, Branford and Kenny claimed that Wynton fired them. But Wynton said, "How can you fire someone who has another job?" He told his brother and Kenny, "You guys are going with Sting. I have to keep my band going." With only half a band left, Wynton had a terrible problem. How could he keep his dates?

The breakup was painful for Wynton. He didn't want it to happen, but Branford felt he needed to leave his brother. Sting's group was a way for Branford to step out of his brother's shadow. And Branford had the ability and wanted to play pop music, although he loved jazz. Wynton asked his own manager to arrange the new contract for Branford with Sting. "Take care of my brother," Wynton told his manager. When his manager hung up the phone, he meditated on how humane Wynton was to say that.

"Take care of my brother."

It took a long time for the rift between the brothers to heal. Jeff Watts, who stayed with Wynton's group, thought Wynton was actually heartbroken. Wynton missed playing with Branford. It took Wynton a while to form a new group with people he could trust to share his music. "A group turns out to be a family thing," Jeff explained.

Both Wynton and Branford eventually benefited from the breakup. Branford went on to lead his own groups, earn critical praise, act in movies, lead the "Tonight Show" band on television, and take an executive job at Sony Music, which owned Columbia Records. Wynton began to explore the jazz tradition more. He built a new group, added people to it, and taught young musicians all the time while he traveled around the world to play music. He invited Marcus Roberts, a blind pianist, to take over Kenny Kirkland's job. Wynton had been keeping track of Marcus and guiding him for years.

And Wynton became a man of the world, making close friends in all the countries he visited. In Marciac, France, the city erected a statue of him. The schoolchildren he coached in music there loved Wynton.

Wherever he went, he visited schools—without pay—and listened to children play their instruments. Some of the children were so inspired that they committed themselves to a career in music. And jazz had become so popular, after Wynton's career and tireless work had opened the doors for many young jazz musicians, that the youngsters could look forward to finding jobs as musicians. Compact discs, too, were helping to boost sales for jazz. CDs were replacing long-playing records, and everyone was buying the latest technology. And Wynton was fulfilling his own promise as a dedicated, high-minded musician. He stood far above most of the people he knew and worked with.

CHAPTER FOUR

THE CALL FROM LINCOLN CENTER

On the road, Wynton helped Marcus Roberts, the blind member of his group. And Wynton's quartet had great successes with albums and performances. Wynton's father sent some of his pupils to Wynton, who coached and advised them. Some were finally hired for his group. It eventually grew to become a sextet, then a septet. And Wynton increasingly drew on the happy, traditional music of New Orleans and the swing era for inspiration.

The public's interest in jazz kept growing. George Weisman, chairman of the board of Lincoln Center, went to a jazz concert one night in 1987 near his home in suburban Rye, New York. The audience cheered for the performances of such fine jazz pianists as Marian McPartland. Weisman, who loved classical music, had never seen wealthy people—"balding, greying, and WASPy" as he described them—react to jazz that way before. "They tore the place apart," he said. He remembered how much he had liked jazz as a young man, when he had gone to jazz clubs once in a while.

Lincoln Center's directors had been trying to think of a way to attract audiences to one of their theaters. Alice Tully Hall was dark during the summers. Weisman went to the office and said, "Bring in jazz." So Nat Leventhal, president of Lincoln Center, asked Alina Bloomgarden to plan a Classical Jazz Festival for Alice Tully Hall.

"Bring in jazz."

Alina, director of Visitors Services, had the job of attracting and welcoming new audiences to Lincoln Center. She had already thought of bringing jazz to Lincoln Center. She had fallen in love with jazz at the Jazz Cultural Theater, a performance space and school founded by jazz pianist Barry Harris in New York City. In the early 1980s, she had told Leventhal: "Jazz is a great American art form. We could have a role to play in how it's received and respected in its own country the way it's respected in Europe and all over the world. We could present jazz the way we present classical music, with informative program notes, thematic programs, repertorial programming."

Now Leventhal told her to go ahead. She

sought the help of Dorthaan Kirk, the widow of a highly regarded reeds player. In February, Alina and Dorthaan began planning three concerts for August —a concert by women musicians; a tribute to Charlie "Bird" Parker, the great alto saxophonist who helped to found the bebop style; and a tribute to Thelonious Monk, a unique jazz pianist and composer. Someone told Alina, "Call Wynton Marsalis." Alina thought it would be hard to interest him in the program. He was so busy traveling with his group and playing in so many special events. But she knew he would make a perfect artistic advisor and help promote the concerts. "I knew he had a vision for the classicism of jazz, for wearing suits and jackets, and dignifying performances," she said.

"I knew he had a vision for the classicism of jazz."

Wynton loved the idea. He said he would do everything he could to help, but he warned Alina that some people would have reservations about working for him. She told him: "I want you." They signed a contract for him to perform without pay for two years—the festival had a very small budget. Other people at Lincoln Center laughed when she said Wynton Marsalis had signed up. So she circulated his contract. "Everyone started talking to me differently," she said.

Wynton plays an outdoor concert with the
Lincoln Center Jazz Orchestra.

A popular local jazz radio station, WBGO,
helped with publicity. Alina commissioned original artwork for the brochures. Wynton, who kept
traveling with his group, by then a septet, sent
Stanley Crouch to write program notes for Classical Jazz concerts. Stanley had written liner notes
for all Wynton's albums. Wynton didn't perform at
Lincoln Center the first year, but the second year
he made himself available for a couple of concerts,
including one featuring the music of Duke Ellington. Stanley brought in David Berger, an Ellington

scholar, copyist, and music transcriber. David transcribed Ellington's music from recordings.

Wynton, David, Alina, and Stanley met to put an orchestra together. Wynton said to David, "What's your concept of how you want to perform this music?" David said he wanted to perform the pieces, but he didn't want anyone to imitate exactly the way Duke's band had played. Wynton said, "Great. That's exactly how I feel. I like this guy." Then he left to keep a pressing commitment. He had so many.

He recorded an album called *The Majesty of the Blues*, with veteran New Orleans players plus members of his septet. Some of the music was completely influenced by New Orleans music, such as the "Happy Feet Blues," part of the traditional Second Line funeral music. (Brass bands play dirges on the way to a cemetery, but on the way back, they play joyous, swinging, religious songs. Only New Orleans has a Second Line tradition.)

At the next meeting with Stanley and Alina, Wynton asked David which musicians he wanted to play in the band. David named "outrageous" people, said Wynton, musicians who would be very difficult to get. Though Wynton didn't even know most of them personally, he promised to get them for David. And Wynton did just that. "It was a dream come true," David said. "All these Duke

Ellington band guys showed up, my heroes from my childhood."

Critics gave the performance great reviews. The next year, the orchestra did more Ellington concerts. And the directors of Lincoln Center became enamored of Wynton Marsalis. He was so articulate and intelligent when he attended their meetings and explained the importance of jazz and its place in the cultural life of America and the world.

Wynton brought along Stanley Crouch and their mentor, Albert Murray. Stanley and Al Murray also spoke at meetings about jazz at Lincoln Center. "They were the philosophers and historians who sort of gave the institutional history to jazz and also to its place in society. They repeated or reinforced what Wynton said . . . And Wynton would say, 'Yeah, man,' and 'Right on,' and agree with them," George Weisman recalled.

The program was so successful that Lincoln Center decided to turn Classical Jazz into a year-round jazz program called Jazz at Lincoln Center. A man named Rob Gibson, who produced the Atlanta Jazz Festival and ran many other jazz programs in Atlanta, was hired to become executive producer. Alina was upset that she didn't get the job, but she knew the change was made in the interest of the success of the program. She didn't hold any grudge against Wynton. She had grown fond of Stanley and Wynton.

She saw that Wynton was a positive, driven man about his work, always doing something. Although his pronouncements and teachings about the joy of jazz made him seem extremely optimistic to many people, she didn't think he actually was. To her, he sometimes seemed to have the weight of the world on his shoulders. "If you know him personally," Alina said, "you know he's not always positive because he has an amazing amount of responsiblity that he manages. In all the years I've known him, he was always managing a band. You have to be a psychologist par excellence to do that. And he's always trying to create. He's also dealing with corporate situations. And then he's dealing with the public. He complained a lot . . . about all the things he had to coordinate, that kind of thing . . . He and Stanley give each other an earful."

His personal life wasn't given any priority. "He knows that about himself. He doesn't make any claim to anyone that he could make it a priority," said Alina. His relationship with Candace Stanley was rocky. They broke up, got back together, and by the time Classical Jazz became Jazz at Lincoln Center, they were living together in a brownstone near the pretty Gramercy Park area of town. Their first son, Wynton, Jr., was born on May 18, 1988, and their second son, Simeon, was born on April 28, 1990. Jazz at Lincoln Center was destined to live happily ever after, but Wynton's little, private family was not.

With his sons Simeon (left) and Wynton, Jr. (right)

CHAPTER FIVE

WYNTON BECOMES A SUPERSTAR

It's a bird; it's a plane; no, it's Wynton Marsalis hopping into planes, buses, and cars to keep dates all around the country and the world. Once a plane flying at 33,000 feet (10,000 meters) made a terrifying 20,000 foot (6,200 m) drop with Wynton aboard. It managed to pull out of the dive, but after that Wynton tried to travel by land whenever possible. That didn't happen often, though, because he had so many far-flung commitments.

On October 22, 1990, *Time* magazine featured Wynton on the cover with the headline "The New Jazz Age." He had just turned 29 years old. The magazine called him the inspiration for a renaissance in jazz. He was one of the few jazz musicians ever to appear on *Time*'s cover. That was a high point in his career. The magazine named 15 budding stars who owed their opportunities to Wynton's successes, including his brother Branford.

Before he was 30, Wynton and his music were featured on the cover of Time *magazine.*

The magazine's writer asked Wynton about his earlier criticisms of Miles Davis for playing fusion. Wynton excused himself on the grounds of his youth. "I was like 19 or something, man—you know, wild. I didn't care," he said. Pianist Billy Taylor, a famous elder statesman of jazz, defended Wynton as the most important young spokesman for jazz. "His opinions are well-founded. Some people earlier took umbrage at what he said, but the important thing is that he could back it up with his horn."[1]

Actually, Wynton never mellowed in his views of Miles's decision to play rock. He and Miles said angry things about each other to reporters. Once at a festival in Canada, Wynton was so annoyed about an insulting remark made by Miles and published in a newspaper that Wynton walked uninvited onto a bandstand where Miles was playing. Wynton started to play. Miles stopped his band, and Wynton had to leave.

None of this publicity hurt Miles or Wynton, however. Miles always kept the haunting, eerie tone that legions of fans worshiped and young trumpeters imitated. And Wynton's successes went beyond his family background and even his own touch of genius and brilliance on his horn. David Berger gave a fine explanation: "He just has got so much energy. He truly has charisma. There's no question about it. It's just excess, positive energy, and he gives it off. It makes people feel good being around him. His attitude is that he'll dream of. something and make it happen. And he does that. And he makes you feel—I could do that too."

> **"His attitude is that he'll dream of something and make it happen."**

Wynton and Rob Gibson met at all hours of the day and night to plan the Jazz at Lincoln Center lectures, films, concerts, and tours. Wynton still traveled on the road with his highly praised septet, but he devoted some time to playing for the Lincoln Center program and composing original works. Nat Leventhal, president of Lincoln Center, wondered how Wynton and Rob could stay up all night working and then work during the day too. Nat decided it must be because they were young. But Wynton always had an uncanny ability to sleep only a couple of hours a night and keep going.

Wynton took on many extra assignments apart from his work with his group and Lincoln Center. He played for a concert for young people involving the cartoon character, Snoopy. The writer for the show was Murray Horwitz, who had begun his career as a clown with Ringling Brothers Barnum & Bailey Circus. To start work on the Snoopy show, Murray treated Wynton to an opera

At home in his New York apartment, Wynton works on a composition for ballet.

the day before he played Charles Mingus's music in a concert at Wolftrap. Wynton was already involved in recording his album, "Crescent City Christmas Card." Then Murray invited Wynton to play in a re-creation of an early jazz band leader's concert at Carnegie Hall. That was James Reese Europe's Clef Club Orchestra concert.

Walking to Wynton's townhouse together in the rain after a rehearsal, Murray and Wynton came up with an idea for a radio series about jazz. Murray was director of jazz, classical music, and entertainment at NPR by then. Wynton kept saying over and over, "What makes the music what it is?" That night the men may have come up with the radio series title, "Making the Music." It grew to have 26 parts, which the men planned during several years in the early 1990s. Wynton composed a theme song, Murray wrote the series, and Wynton revised and reshaped it.

"Wynton was great at pushing everybody to think and work hard and find ways to do something in a fresh way . . . Wynton would say, 'Why not try this?' and he was right," Horwitz recalled. "It wasn't always something that cost more money. It was just about thinking a little differently. And you won't hear anything bad about him from me. It became real clear early on that he was one of the smartest people I ever worked with in my life.

I told people, 'This guy is the real thing. He's going to leave all of us in the dust,'" Murray said.

"We asked ourselves: What do we want to achieve with this show on fusion? Or bebop? What do we want to say about Ellington? If we had three or four things to say about Thelonious Monk, what would we say about him? Then we fleshed those answers out with Wynton." Though busy with other projects, Wynton worked very hard on the series, sometimes staying up nearly all night to work by telephone. "We held the phone up at the speakers to play music for him," Murray recalled.

> **"This guy is the real thing. He's going to leave all of us in the dust."**

In 1994, they went into production for the start of the shows for 1995. Sometimes Murray and his production crew chased Wynton to other cities—such as Chico, California, and Atlanta, Georgia. And Wynton went to NPR headquarters in Washington, D.C., where he liked to walk the halls and look into people's offices. "I know most people live their lives this way, but I live my life in hotel rooms and buses," he said.

"At NPR, he went to work in an office every day," Murray recalled. "People loved him. The classical people got the benefit too. He talked to the NPR board one day. He was really part of the family."

Murray was delighted with the series. "If you listen to all 26 parts, you'll know a lot about jazz," he said. The Peabody Awards people agreed. In the spring of 1996, Horwitz and Wynton learned that the series had won a Peabody—the highest award in broadcasting. To attend the awards ceremony, seven people connected with the show went from Washington to New York "and crashed on Wynton's floor," Murray recalled. "Wynton made gumbo for us, and he and I made the acceptance speech."

Wynton received a fee for the series. People called Murray from Lincoln Center and Wynton's manager's office to ask: "What are you doing?" There was so much work and so little money—perhaps a $20,000 budget for years of work by Wynton. Whatever Wynton earned, his manager took care of and invested it for him. Wynton was quite a wealthy man by then from all his enterprises. He and Candace had split up by the time the series aired and won an award. Their townhouse was sold, and Wynton moved to a condominium at Lincoln Center.

Candace went on to build herself a new life. Wynton took care of his sons when he was in town. Sometimes he took them on the road. Otherwise,

Candace raised them with her new husband and their two children, a girl and a boy. Certified as a teacher of very young children, she taught in the public school system in a New York suburb.

Beginning in 1992, Wynton often appeared on regular broadcasts of a radio show called "Jazz at Lincoln Center." Some of the tapes eventually submitted for consideration for the Peabody Award were excerpts from concert performances of New Orleans pianist-composer Jelly Roll Morton, Thelonious Monk, Wynton, and others playing a wide selection of the music broadcast on the shows. Some critics had been upset that Wynton played Jelly Roll's music from the early years of the 20th century. They said Wynton could have chosen more modern music. But Wynton's interpretation of Jelly Roll's music was exhilarating and uplifting. Wynton had made a brilliant choice. The Lincoln Center radio series, too, would win a Peabody by 1997.

Probably Wynton's best-known exploit in broadcasting, was "Marsalis on Music," because it was televised in a four-part Public Broadcasting System series. In July 1994, Wynton traveled with a crew of about 25 Sony video producers, directors, recording engineers, camera men, and stagehands to Tanglewood at Lenox, Massachusetts. They set up shop in a red barn across the street from the main festival grounds.

The television series "Marsalis on Music" gave Wynton a chance to do one of his favorite things—help kids to love music.

The production disrupted the usually calm scene there for two weeks. But the shows, aired in 1995, charmed television audiences. Wynton, playing with his own group, explained aspects of jazz history and performances. Conductor Seiji

Ozawa and the Boston Symphony Orchestra, plus classical cellist Yo-Yo Ma and his cello quartet played there, too.

Not only children but adults loved the shows. One show, entitled "Souza to Satchmo," taught how music evolved from classical to Souza marches to Louis Armstrong. As just one element on this video, Wynton explained how syncopation meant accents on unexpected beats. For illustrations of ensemble playing, he used musicians from the Lincoln Center Jazz Orchestra and the Liberty Brass Band with traditional New Orleans clarinetist Dr. Michael White. Wynton showed how various instruments played their own melody lines in their own spaces—clarinets on top, trumpets and saxophones in the middle, and trombones on a lower plane.

For another show, "Listening for Clues: Marsalis on Form," Wynton taught about the forms of music and showed how different types of music related to one another. He used the classical sonata form and contrasted it with the 32-bar American standard song form. He had uncanny ways of making clear what he was trying to teach. For example, he reminded kids that their schooldays had a certain schedule with classes, and weekends began with cartoons on television. If they knew what usually happened on a weekend, they could identify the day. And "knowing the form (of a piece of music) means you know what is going to happen. You can recognize it," he said. And recognition enhanced the pleasure of listening to music.

To teach the sonata form, he used an incredibly whimsical analogy: A child goes to a pet store to buy a puppy but can afford only a hamster. So he buys the hamster and puts it in a cage. That's the statement of the sonata's theme. Then the hamster gets loose from its cage and runs away. The child chases it all over the store until he finally catches up with it. That ends the second part of the sonata, called the *fantasia*. Then the restatement of the theme begins and proceeds to the end of the sonata.

To teach the 32-bar American song form, Wynton and his jazz orchestra played "I Got Rhythm" by George Gershwin, and showed how the tune was divided into four sections of eight bars each. And for the show called "Why Toes Tap," Wynton taught that rhythm is the most basic element of music. Without rhythm, there's no music. You can't even get from one note to another, because the change from one note to another sets up a rhythm. "Music is organized sound in time," he said. And for a show called "Tackling the Monster," Wynton and Yo-Yo Ma talked about the skills of practicing. Their 12-point program could be applied to nearly any job in life.

They set up such principles as: Seek out a good teacher who knows what you're supposed to be doing; write out a schedule for your daily practice, so you know what you are planning to do that day. Set long-term goals for yourself, so you know what you want to accomplish over a period of time. Concentrate when you practice, and if you can't keep your mind on what you're doing, stop for a while and come back to it so that you can clear your head, focus on your task, and feel good about yourself. Take your time. You may not be able to play a piece fast at first, so practice it slowly and gain speed. Practice everything as if you were singing. That technique will help you express yourself. Don't be too hard on yourself. Don't feel bad about making mistakes, because you learn from mistakes. The only people who don't make mistakes are the ones who aren't practicing or doing anything. On and on the lessons went. The entertaining, profoundly instructive series earned him another Peabody Award on May 6, 1996, at the Waldorf Astoria Hotel.

Last but not least, Wynton started a concert series called "Jazz for Young People" at Alice Tully Hall on several Saturdays a year. It became one of Jazz at Lincoln Center's most popular and suc-

Wynton coaches a young trumpeter
backstage at Lincoln Center.

cessful events, with topics such as "What is Swing?" and "Who Is Louis Armstrong?" and "What is Cool?"

Wynton opened his "What Is Cool?" lecture by introducing his group—seven members of the Lincoln Center Jazz Orchestra. He waited for a while to mention his own name, then said, "I give my own name plenty of space. That's cool." He explained how food can be cooked over a high flame or a low flame. The low flame is the cool way to cook and just as thorough and intense a method as a high

The "Jazz for Young People" series at Lincoln Center was fun for Wynton and his audience.

flame. So the low flame is very deceptive, he explained. Finding himself talking into the wrong microphone, he picked up his papers from the lectern in front of it and switched to the right microphone. "Now you don't see me rushing and hurrying to get from one mike to another," he said. "When you make a mistake, take your

"When you make a mistake, take your time. That's your first lesson in being cool today."

time. That's your first lesson in being cool today."
The audience, adults and children, roared.

"To be cool, you have to be relaxed. Don't rush
from place to place." He went on to relate his ideas
to music, explaining that cool music is played at
slow or medium tempos. And cool musicians fig-
ure out ways to make fast tempos sound slow. "To
mess up, turn the music up loud. That's popular
music," Wynton said, taking the opportunity to
criticize one of his greatest annoyances.

Soon he moved on to talk about musicians
revered for their coolness. One was Lester Young,
a tenor saxophonist who became famous in Count
Basie's first band. "Lester may have been the
coolest musician who ever lived," Wynton said.
Lester didn't jump around. "He had soft eyes.
That was important," Wynton explained. A cool
person has to have soft eyes, or else his eyes might
look cold and hard, and that's not cool.

"And (Lester) played in a soft, lyrical way.
The lyrical way to play is with embellishments—
but without verboseness or florid decorations,"
Wynton explained. It's the difference between a
man handing a woman a bouquet of flowers and
saying, "I thought of you," or saying "Take this."
The audience laughed heartily, loving Wynton,
learning from him, from his romance with
metaphors in his teaching style. Musical knowl-
edge became fun for them, as it was for Wynton.

Wynton went on to explain the subtlety and introspection of the cool approach to jazz and showed a film clip of Lester Young, who always held his saxophone at a tipped angle. Wynton pointed out that Lester, playing an intense, soulful blues, had been holding a cigarette between two fingers and didn't get burned. "And you knew he wouldn't get burned," Wynton said, "because he was cool."

Wynton went on to talk about hot and fiery bebop—not a cool style of music—and then the cool generation of musicians who followed bebop. Miles Davis was the most famous of them, with his spare themes played in the middle register of the trumpet. He had an introspective approach and sound and no vibrato. Wynton demonstrated Miles's haunting sound, using a little Harmon mute attached to the bell of his trumpet. It produced the opposite of happy, hot, New Orleans music. And Wynton went on to talk about the cool, or laid-back, California sound of baritone saxophonist Gerry Mulligan, and then the cool, relaxed, lyrical, melodic music of the Brazilians and their softly swinging *bossa nova* beat.

These were just some of the projects that Wynton fit into his brimming schedule.

CHAPTER SIX

CONTROVERSIES AND VICTORIES

Despite his professional successes, Wynton's personal life wasn't running smoothly. After he and Candace broke up, he had a collection of girlfriends. One of them, a well-known and beautiful actress, Victoria Rowell, became pregnant. She and Wynton had no plans to marry. Since she worked in a daytime soap opera, she lived in the Los Angeles area. Their son, Jasper Armstrong, lived with her, and Wynton visited him when he could. Jasper came to see him too. Sometimes Wynton took care of his three sons at once. He was great at playing with them, soothing their fears, and feeding them.

Once, when Jasper started crying, Wynton shouted even louder than his son. Jasper thought that was so much fun, he started smiling.

For Christmas 1997, when Jasper was two years old, Wynton took him to spend the holidays with Ellis and Dolores in New Orleans. And Wynton looked forward to the day when Jasper would be old enough to stay with him for long periods of time in New York. The birth of that son made Wynton's already hectic life even more complicated. Certainly some of his other girlfriends were very upset.

Wynton could always rely upon his loyal male friends for relaxed company. Sometimes they set aside time to travel with him when he had concerts to play, speeches to make, and classes to teach in far-flung cities. They drove across the country, laughing and joking, stopping at good restaurants and basketball courts for recreation. Over the years, Wynton had forged strong friendships. One good friend was the doctor who had introduced him to Candace Stanley. Another was a policeman in Chicago. Still another was a tennis pro who had grown up playing trumpet with Wynton in schools and orchestras in New Orleans. And a businessman in the auto industry in Detroit, who loved jazz, became a fan, and developed into a close friend. A keen observer of business deals, that friend surmised that Wynton had become a millionaire through his hard work, his earning power, and the wise investments of his manager.

Young musicians constantly visited Wynton's condominium in New York. He taught them about

Outside his home in New Orleans

music, and they played basketball with him for exercise and fun at a court near his house.

But most of his social life revolved around the demands of his career in music. In 1994, it became clear that Jazz at Lincoln Center was a great critical and financial success. The directors of Lincoln Center decided to elevate the year-round program to become a major part of the center's productions. That meant jazz would have equal status at Lincoln Center with the other great art forms, such as the opera, the ballet, and the symphony. Jazz would get the recognition it deserved as a great, original American art form. Wynton was going to devote much more of his time to Jazz at Lincoln Center now. As artistic director of the new jazz program, he would lead the Lincoln Center Jazz Orchestra in person and take it on tour.

So in December 1994, Wynton took his septet into the Village Vanguard, a historic club in New York, for the last time. He disbanded the group, but he took many of its musicians into the Lincoln Center Jazz Orchestra.

Wynton, Rob Gibson, Stanley Crouch, and Albert Murray were overjoyed about the new jazz program. So were legions of other jazz fans. But some people were very upset, primarily because they had no authority over the Jazz at Lincoln Center programs. These critics wanted to have at least some choice in the music and musicians presented at the center. Of course, these critics—and musicians, too—had no right to make choices. Also, Wynton asserted his position and taste forcefully. He wrote letters to the editors of magazines that criticized him when he thought the criticisms were unfair or uninformed. Fearless by nature, extremely sensitive to criticism, and even happy to fight about issues and ideas at times, he never shrank from a debate or a confrontation.

Among the program's many activities, Jazz at Lincoln Center taped all performances beginning in 1991. Thousands of tapes existed by 1998. Rob and Wynton wanted to make their archive available to future generations. Another important enterprise was the annual Essentially Ellington High School Band Competition and Festival. It was created to make Ellington's music available to high school students who could then play it in their bands. In his travels, Wynton was upset that high school bands didn't play music that he thought would teach them how to play or understand music. He felt they would learn a lot more by playing Ellington's music. So he helped invent a grand remedy.

The festival began in 1996 as a Tri-State Festival in the New York City area. Then it expanded to include schools in the Northeast and mid-Atlantic States. By 1998, it grew to encompass schools from 26 states east of the Mississippi

*At a Tri-State Festival, Wynton gives
high school students some guidance.*

River. And Wynton and Rob hoped to make the
competition even larger. The finalists came to
New York City and competed against one another.
Each band brought its well-wishers and cheering
sections. Their enthusiasm welled up in the hall
repeatedly. They even cheered for the rival bands
they liked.

In the 1998 competition, Branford Marsalis
served as one of the judges. After the competition
was over, he showed up on stage to play with the
Lincoln Center Jazz Orchestra. And he was the

High school students get personal instruction from Wynton.

only one of the musicians who didn't wear the orchestra's uniform. But the rift between Wynton and Branford had healed. They often worked together both on and off the bandstands.

After Jazz at Lincoln Center officially became a full member of the arts program in July 1996, the number of concerts, events, and educational programs kept growing. The Jazz at Lincoln Center Orchestra toured the world, presenting the music of Duke Ellington, Thelonious Monk, John Coltrane, and other famed players and composers of jazz history. Wynton loved Ellington above all. Each year, the tours attracted larger audiences

The Lincoln Center Jazz Orchestra

and visited more cities and countries. The orchestra's repertoire also included original music by Wynton. Some of the pieces were commissioned by Lincoln Center. The rumor was that a commission could pay a composer $20,000.

That was another bone of contention between Wynton and his critics. They thought Wynton was getting too many commissions, while other musicians, particularly experimental musicians, weren't getting any. Furthermore, because the

Lincoln Center Jazz Orchestra had 4 or 5 white musicians out of about 16 players, critics said that Wynton and the Jazz at Lincoln Center program were racist. However, the number of white players was not a bad proportion, when one realized that jazz orchestras had, at one time, been totally segregated. And furthermore, in the classical world, it was still usual to find all-white orchestras. Wynton and Rob pointed out that many of the people working in positions of authority at Lincoln Center, such as David Berger, the Ellington transcriber, were white. And Rob Gibson himself was white. He described himself as proud of his WASP background.

The white musicians in the Jazz at Lincoln Center orchestra tried to defend Wynton. None of them had ever experienced the slightest hint of racism in their dealings with him or anyone else at Lincoln Center.

But it was true that Jazz at Lincoln Center staged tributes to some of the great jazz innovators and composers, and only one night had been totally devoted to a white composer—Gerry Mulligan. Other white musicians and composers had been featured to an important degree as well as songs by many white composers. It was also true that the program had never dedicated a night to the great jazz clarinetist Benny Goodman, who had been a pioneer in integrating jazz groups. He had led a landmark integrated concert at Carnegie Hall in 1938, presenting some of the greatest white and African-American jazz musicians in the world at that time. Rob Gibson tried to defend the omission of a celebration of Goodman's music by saying the clarinetist hadn't written anything. And the charts Goodman used had often been written by black musicians, composers, and arrangers.

To answer accusations that he was racist, or that he didn't use enough white musicians, or that he hired musicians on the basis of friendship, Wynton talked to writer Thomas Sancton for an article in *Jazz Times* magazine in the summer of 1997. "It's a response to the perception of me using power the way that I want to use it as artistic director of Jazz at Lincoln Center, to present my vision of it, which is what I am hired to do. And that's something that makes a lot of critics uncomfortable—much more than they would be in another field. You can be sure that other artistic directors don't have to put up with that."[1]

Wynton was also criticized for excluding musicians who played electronic instruments, and jazz-rock fusion, and the avant-garde or so-called experimental players. Jazz at Lincoln Center was setting standards and parameters for the type of jazz that Wynton wanted to feature. It was always traditional, mainstream, acoustic music. His tastes set critics and musicians to fighting with one another—usually just with words. But the arguments were heated. The public knew and cared very little about the controversies and kept showing up for the brilliant concerts of the kind of music that had attracted fans to jazz in the first place.

Rob Gibson said that all the other art forms presented at Lincoln Center—and artistic groups in general—set their own standards and featured the music of their leaders and artistic directors. It was not unusual for Jazz at Lincoln Center to do that. But controversies still raged over Wynton's choices of music.

Jazz at Lincoln Center wasn't perfect. Wynton Marsalis was not the greatest jazz composer who ever lived—though he was very good and sometimes great, and he was an unsurpassed master of his instrument. However both the program and Wynton were still young—and both were very exciting. Rob Gibson compared the program to a tall building. He said the program was like an elevator that had risen from the ground to one of the lower floors and still had a long way to go to reach the top. He and Wynton were devoting their lives to the growth and rise of the program.

Wynton personally continued to receive constant attention in the media and honorary doctorates. They came from such schools as Rutgers University and Yale University, whose scholarship he had passed up as a teenager. He was appointed to prestigious arts councils, among them the New York State Council on the Arts in 1997. The greatest of his honors was the Pulitzer Prize, which he won in 1997.

Wynton had actually composed his Pulitzer prize-winning oratorio, *Blood on the Fields*, in 1994, when it had its premiere in New York City. One critic, Chip Deffaa, attended the premiere and gave the long piece a very favorable review in the *New York Post* on April 4, 1994. "Despite some tedious stretches—the impact of the 3½ hour-long-work would be heightened by tough editing—this is the 32-year-old Marsalis's most ambitious, adventurous, and impressive work yet. Some segments are devastatingly brilliant on every level: music, lyrics, arrangement, and execution. This is Marsalis's first composition for his big band. I wish he hadn't waited so long to write for a big band, because he has an enormous contribution to make. The introductory bars alone were as strongly original as anything I've heard in years. His uses of color show he has learned well the lessons of Ellington . . . Marsalis's own solo contributions on trumpet, hot and inventive, also commanded attention . . ."[2]

Many critics seemed to have missed that performance. Wynton didn't record the oratorio until 1995. Released on a CD in 1996, the year for which it won the Pulitzer Prize, it was a work in words and music using the history of slavery as an allegory for the human condition and the confusion a person can feel about his or her identity. He scheduled a tour in the United States and Europe to perform the difficult music in 1996. It used up a great deal of his and his orchestra's energy. His mother worried about how hard the tours were. She worried, too, about the amount of criticism her son had to confront in general. Critics were divided about the value of Wynton's oratorio. He performed it for the first time at Lincoln Center on February 24, 1997.

Fine reviews were published in the *Chicago Tribune, USA Today*, and the *Los Angeles Times*. Howard Reich of the *Chicago Times* called the piece "Wynton's victory." Not only did Reich appreciate the music, but he praised the award going to *Blood on the Fields* because it honored the American art of jazz improvisation. (Duke Ellington had been passed over for a Pulitzer Prize strictly on the basis of his racial background about 30 years earlier. The honor was very late in going to jazz or any jazz composer.)

"Wynton's victory."

One of the worst reviews came from Gary Giddins of the *Village Voice*, who said the oratorio was too long. He didn't like the music at all. And he simply thought Wynton had a nerve. Giddins had become increasingly critical of Wynton over the years and didn't think Wynton had the right to the Pulitzer in 1996, since the piece had first been performed and recorded in earlier years. (Giddins, normally a brilliant and prize-winning critic, had the unhappy memory of watching his own fine, ambitious jazz orchestra fail; he had launched it in the 1980s, just when Lincoln Center's jazz program got started. Giddins once admitted in an article in the *Voice* that he felt very bad about the situation.)

Branford Marsalis wrote a letter to the editor of the *Village Voice*, published on July 17, 1997, saying that the Giddins review made Branford realize "how pathetic critical evaluation of modern music is today . . ." And "Though I do not expect Giddins to understand or appreciate music as complex as *Blood on the Fields*, an unjust music review anywhere is a threat to just reviews everywhere."[3] Giddins added his last lick, implying that Branford's letter was motivated by brotherly love.

Hundreds of events filled the calendar for Jazz at Lincoln Center, more with each passing year. In the winter of 1998, it was announced that the Coliseum building at Columbus Circle and 59th Street, near Lincoln Center, was going to be torn down. A new concert hall and rehearsal space would be built there. The hall would be used by Jazz at Lincoln Center. So the news was absolutely great.

Criticisms occasionally still surfaced about Wynton—sometimes in print, sometimes in conversations between musicians or critics. But Wynton's ideas and methods had created the basis of a brilliant future for jazz—and hadn't hurt his own career at all, no matter what changes might be made in his programs one day.

Wynton told a reporter that he had been motivated by a desire to help jazz musicians like his father. They had so much to give and found so little acceptance. When he was growing up, Wynton had seen their suffering firsthand. And Wynton wanted to make older musicians proud of him. Despite all the controversies that had beset him, he felt he had accomplished his mission. "I think it," he told reporter Ed Bradley softly and earnestly on "60 Minutes" on CBS.[4]

Another writer said to Branford Marsalis, "Wynton is a lightning rod for a lot of criticism of various aspects of the social order of the country." What did Branford think about the way Wynton ran Lincoln Center? And what would Branford do if he was running it?

"I wouldn't," Branford said. "I wouldn't want that job for all the tea in China . . . A lot of people could do it, but not as good as he can do it." Branford thought it was a virtual miracle that Wynton could combine his role as a creative artist and virtuoso with the job of dealing with a great corporation such as Lincoln Center. Wynton had "sophisticated social graces," Branford said. Branford hadn't thought it was a job that Wynton had dreamed he would grow up to do. "But he can do anything well. What can't he do well? . . I think that what he has done so far is wonderful."[5]

> **"What can't he do well? . . I think that what he has done so far is wonderful."**

Putting it all into perspective for another reporter, Wynton said in 1998, "I've had a great time out here."[6]

Whether he is performing, composing, or teaching, Wynton brings passion and excellence to making music.

CHRONOLOGY

1961	Wynton Marsalis is born in New Orleans on October 18.
1973	Wynton becomes serious about playing the trumpet and practices all the time.
1978	Wynton leaves home to spend the summer at Tanglewood Music Festival, Lenox, MA. In September, he moves to New York City, attends Juilliard School of Music, and begins playing with Art Blakey and the Jazz Messengers.
1979	Wynton formally joins Blakey's group and tours the world.
1980	He makes his first commercial recordings with Blakey's group.
1981	In August, his recording career as a leader begins with Columbia. His first album, *Wynton Marsalis*, recorded just before his 20th birthday, comes out.
1983	He wins a Grammy for Best Jazz Instrumental Performance, Soloist, for *Think of One*, his second album, and Best Classical Performance, Instrumental, Soloist or

Soloists with Orchestras, for "Concerto for Trumpet and Orchestra in E Flat Major," L. Mozart, composer.

1984   Wynton wins a Grammy for Best Jazz Instrumental Performance, Soloist, for *Hot House Flowers*, his third jazz album, and for Best Classical Performance, Instrumental, for *Wynton Marsalis*, for Baroque Music for Trumpet.

1985   Wynton receives two more Grammys for Best Jazz Instrumental Performance, Soloist, and Best Jazz Instrumental Performance, Group, for *Black Codes from the Underground.*

1986   Branford Marsalis strikes out on his own to focus on his career. *J. Mood* wins a Grammy for Wynton and his group.

1987   Wynton is invited to act as artistic director for a new, week-long summer program called Classical Jazz at Lincoln Center. He and his group win another Grammy, for *Marsalis Standard Time, Vol. I.*

1990   Classical Jazz becomes a year-round program at Lincoln Center

1995   Wynton makes four videos at Tanglewood Music Festival with conductor Seizi Ozawa and cellist Yo Yo Ma. The series wins a Peabody, the highest award in broadcasting.

1996   "Making the Music," a 26-part radio series on jazz, wins a Peabody. Jazz at Lincoln Center becomes a full constituent, having equal footing with opera, ballet, and symphony.

1997   Wynton wins the Pulitzer Prize for his jazz oratorio *Blood on the Fields.*

GLOSSARY

acoustic refers to music that does not use electronic instruments

barometer a standard to measure something by

citation a formal statement of a person's achievements

conservatory a school for music or the arts

ensemble a group of musicians or actors who perform together

fusion popular music combining different styles, such as jazz and rock

legacy something handed down from one generation to another

spirituality the quality of being sensitive to spiritual or religious matters

staunch faithful; steadfast in loyalty to something

virtuoso a highly skilled performer, especially a musician

CHAPTER THREE

1. *Stereo Review*, New York, May 1982.
2. Richard Sudhalter, *New York Post*, March 5, 1982.
3. Interview with Wynton Marsalis by Leslie Gourse.

CHAPTER FIVE

1. *Time* magazine, Oct. 22, 1990.

CHAPTER SIX

1. "A Conversation With Wynton Marsalis," a question-and-answer piece by Thomas Sancton, *Jazz Times* magazine, March 1997.
2. "Marsalis's 'Blood' Is Full of Life," by Chip Deffaa, *New York Post*, April 4, 1994.
3. *Village Voice*, July 17, 1997, Letters to the Editor.
4. "60 Minutes," CBS-TV, an interview with Ed Bradley, Nov. 26, 1995.
5. Interview with Branford Marsalis by Leslie Gourse, 1998.
6. Interview with Wynton Marsalis by Leslie Gourse, 1998.

BOOKS

Marsalis, Wynton, *Marsalis on Music*, W.W. Norton and Company, 1995.

Marsalis, Wynton, *Sweet Swing Blues on the Road*, W.W. Norton and Company, 1994.

VIDEOS

Marsalis on Music, 1995
Griot New York, 1991
Trumpet Kings, Jazz Images, Inc., 1985.

INTERNET SITES

Jazz Radio.org
http://www.murraystreet.com/jazzindex.htm
Programming highlights for Jazz at Lincoln Center.

"Making the Music"
http://www.npr.org/programs/mtm/
Website for the 26-part radio production, featuring information about the series, and program listings.

Marsalis on Music Homepage
http://www.wnet.org/archive/mom/homepage.html
This site is an accompaniment to the PBS series. Includes a transcript of an online chat hosted by Wynton, a Music Educator's Guide, and more.

Wynton Marsalis: Columbia Jazz
http://www.sonymusic.com/artists/Wynton Marsalis
Overview of Wynton's Volume 5 of *Standard Time, Vol. 5: The Midnight Blues*, with biography, images, and discography on Sony Music.

Wynton Marsalis: Jazz Musician
http:www.achievement.org/autodoc/page/mar0-pro-1
Profile, biography, and an interview with Wynton.

Wynton Marsalis Online at Jazz World.com
http://www.jazzworld.com/Artist_Info/wynton-marsalis/
Web page of Wynton Marsalis, with photos, links, artists, discography, current news, and performing schedule.

Young Man with a Horn
http://www.weeklywire.com/ww/11-09-98/Memphis_afea.html
Transcript of an interview with Wynton from the Memphis Flyer.

INDEX

Page numbers in *italics* indicate illustrations.

ABOUT THE AUTHOR

Leslie Gourse has researched and written stories for various media, including CBS and the New York Times. Her articles and stories have appeared in magazines and newspapers, covering general culture, social trends, and music. Her books, including Dizzy Gillespie and the Birth of Bebop, and Blowing on the Changes: The Art of the Jazz Horn Players, have earned high praise from the critics.